In Memory of Brilliance & value

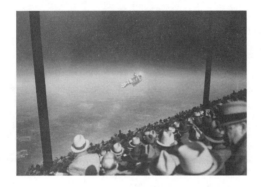

Michael Robins

saturnalia books

Distributed by University Press of New England
Hanover and London

Saturnalia Books
105 Woodside Rd.
Ardmore, PA 19003
info@saturnaliabooks.com

ISBN: 978-0-9915454-8-3
Library of Congress Control Number: 2015945807

Book Design by Saturnalia Books
Printing by Westcan Printing Group, Canada

Cover Art: Joseba Elorza

Distributed by:
University Press of New England
1 Court Street
Lebanon, NH 03766
800-421-1561

Grateful acknowledgment is made to the editors of the following, where versions of these poems first appeared: *Academy of American Poets*, *Arsenic Lobster*, *Bateau*, *Black Tongue Review*, *Court Green*, *Jet Fuel Review*, *Kettle Blue Review*, *The Laurel Review*, *Mantis*, *Matter*, *Mid-American Review*, *Moon City Review*, *Poets for Living Waters*, *POOL*, *Rabbit Light Movies*, *Redactions*, *RHINO*, *Route 9*, *Sakura Review*, *Souvenir*, *Third Coast*, and *The Tusculum Review*.

Contents

Sit in the room. It is true in the moonlight
That it is as if we had never been young.

—Wallace Stevens

I

Like an Arrow that Feels

Candor shoots a wink, heart & pang
when hapless geese shiver through

the turbine & blades. Didn't know
speech was a gander flunked to hell.

We bade swelling in our chair, eyes
blotto, duplicate Tuesday afternoons

woozy & waged toward zero o'clock.
Our mouths wore an array of croon.

Spring swung like an April in waves
foreseeable, feathered, shoring blue.

We'd forgotten our tools for a party
counting highballs, ice, crooked time

hanging on its skinny nail. Honestly,
we hadn't reckoned planting a war.

Many said I love you, many said too
I'll call you when we land. We were

together omens slipped from a note.
We wish we'd made these stories up.

Just a Few Yards Past the Earth

My mind no longer pawed the woods,
no peaks higher than a scissored scarf

nor would I be applause. Landlocked
& cursing, our shushed voices caged,

in what further humor might I begin
purging the trivial, the fading thrush.

Transcripts of such narratives disband
when no stars fly nor nestle the trees.

So nosebleeds, so much for spinning
the trajectory tilted too steep, steeply

bleached, years white then burdening
this origin thinking of me, me, & me.

Hazards sprung in orange vests ahead
& I was amazed by our secrets in sleet

or if the sun broke cloud astoundingly
like weight on the frozen film of rivers.

Body into a flue, soul & plaster to sand
to tiny, swarming ideas with the wind

just as much with our lives. Permit me
arguments of the splendid & wronged

prancing & darted in the lilt of a crow.
Our flags sing even as we move along.

Marathon of Deletions

While that circus leaves the curb
coolly, downpour & declaration

to the drain. Travels rearranged,
rejoiced with the deafening trot

inside fox furs, men minus feet
who nonetheless hymn & sashay.

With luck I'm born & an artist,
devise friends & those irreverent

in a drawer. How often I return
my passport to its own devices,

amateur backing a moving truck
on this day, squarely one day ago

when that hasty boy painted love
ageless & unrequited. Buoyancy,

anniversary in the rattles & spray.
Umbrellas flowered for the storm.

Anecdote of the Flowering Dogwood

She knows no better pronouncing many
when dying turn monarch. Or if many

slump in their hay like sonnets. She says
rock & roll must be restored, this night

runs on moonshine, racooned emotion
sputtering the fumes. The market sucks

so she instructs better death than winter,
all corduroy & jungle gyms, young joys

who cheerfully kill to trophy a ponytail.
Make of her craving a tugboat distressed,

bristling, the mutiny howled as it breaks
even in light, stain-glassed, fully inflamed.

Poem for Beachheads & Briars

Awoken by the immaculate flaw
in my bed. Quietude, hollowed

limbs through which the breeze
still moves. Kicking molecules,

I've come to intuit wavelengths,
how Made in America illustrates

that most blown, charitable days
revolve this walk swept of sand.

Smashed & believing whichever
whim as promise, routed crowd,

scenes becoming then breached.
How I wish to bear the purpose

of men carrying a ladder. Maybe
they rescue the wayfared kitten

or cart the rungs for the woods,
heaved & fetched until each stays.

In the Elegiac Manner

Between meals, they're out digging
filthiness & yellowed leaves. They

nuzzle not in a housedress bouquet
drying on clothespins. Fever soaked

instead, petals ripped in search of X.
Saturday lows wildlife & the gate left

open wide, goodbye Honey I'm out
to see friends. By their black knees,

bootlace governing the tongue, split
& flush they smirch the countryside.

They crane to kiss a child for the bus,
drink the crystal emptied of its glass.

Inside their homes, wrung & within
such rooms the napkin, heart & hand.

Anecdote of the Date Palm

Like these timbers, water leans to bury
me alive, my hood & throat, my mark

that climbs the fuse of a calendar black,
insomniac under the ancient, naked bulb.

Summer sinking to solstice, the marriage
of breath & braid. Chirp, chirp chirping

that script to rewind, redact & rescind.
I remember how scent can spare, mercy

swollen from orange & fevered, spasm
to spur beneath a rib so scavenged clean

& the music racks across the plastic sheet
over my head. To pretend I'm the fruit

in trees, neck of a worried bird wedged,
stemmed in the rosebush. No figments

of my brothers gathered from the flood,
shun in caves, their hatchets for lamplight.

Poem for Degrees & Resistance

For some the sun, & this on the surface
winter lets her kindling go. Strategies

change, people overlay new costumes
to double their kisses perched in a bow.

Metallic ripple, inferno shore, nothing
earthly rises here between I'm sorry

& disaster for some. I am stammering
for glaciers flag farther than conceived.

Some bother, some relax & lying back
welcome the bell of the buckled deck

as though no stony warning can scorch
our hips. Over love the iceberg turns,

mistakes standing if the fellow stands
to leap as the poet before him. Famed,

we're swirling earnestly in facts, some
in a gold watch or watching ourselves

pulled by its chain. Adrift, castaways
waiting for that great rescue to unfold.

Glare in the Human Canvas

Hardly understand by the stars,
stripes they make when my eyes

tilt back, spin. Wild gloaming,
nettles as well as the creek beds

swollen by the rain, the spigot
not a bear storming the grounds.

Many gone & many up hillsides
peeling pavement from the road,

hazed & pure. Lives are floating,
stories stick to them like debris

angered, fickle, ringing forward.
For many the spur flouts frailty

& this weather erodes devotion
from those yet awakened, those

zipped in tents & into the flow
not rumor, the flash & its finish

finally grasped. Southern pride
values its justice swift & carried

away. The radio delivers water,
broadcasts the curtains that near.

I fasten my lids, the constellation
bends & seizes with it these heads.

Song of the Second Fiddle

We pray, migrate west & inscribe
the bloated deer, they who crawl

obliquely like we do. Hammering,
feeling sorry, muttered & arrowed.

We watched women flee the river
& ourselves from the din of the city.

We frame the errant note by spilling
blood. We strip the days of objects,

hope to lengthen stains that pervade
the new valley like vines. Anything

we would do, the war could better,
& whatever we gleaned we'd glean

in lieu of livelihood. We're cadence
advancing the falls & its rocks below.

Outside the Pay-Per-View Museum

Water was pleading for it, fluttered
sheets wrestled in the foam & roar.

Not a herd, it's the string of buffalo
who once grazed coolly. Who wasn't

bewildered by wagons bravely rolled,
fanning the wilds toward a baldness.

No bray of a biplane either, neither
smoke, nor a family who isn't yours.

Hearsay dwindles by cannon & pinch
to precipitation. Cloudsped, equally

fast the horses producing the plains.
They were wheeling, then a caravan

poured forth these children. They're
inching over the hills with grubbing,

boasting wet in a landscape portrait.
It was shot-for-shot. It was sensation.

II

Pseudonymously Yours

We were lustered, nightfall elusive
of description. Fortune shifted red

pastures to green, my platonic eyes
traversing hers in a bathroom mirror.

I can't retrieve her name for colors
consume the tall, bleached dwelling

where she floated angelic at the sink,
akin & high. We held to each other.

Strangers, drained, our poise wasted
trying toothsome words for their size.

I was shoulder, my world advocating
dimness. Mostly my friends petered

briefly, drinking more from the river
than its ineffable flood would allow.

Then my girlfriend slept with another
boy. I was pedaled late, & even later

we spent scores on that roof to make
amends. My blue bicycle everywhere.

After a While It Hurts to Smile

Under the fell of gloss, or as much
glaciered among places you swear

you never lived: Iowa, Clear Lake
where engines stutter in meadows

& lie along the fence. These homes
cough record of yellow land, echo

thistles & catch the banner circling
up over the pageantry of a goldfinch.

Your lowdown acts upon jauntiness,
first person or third. You've come

to steal a plant, pinned the apology
& returned it strong, seasons after.

You revive where the snow melts
back. A kind story that isn't yours,

winter arriving even here or even
flowers at the end of a snaking road.

Poem for Shimmers & Shadowtackle

Cinched the belt over hatred, over
ho-hum hours, their surprises few

& seconds served. Neither do I help
but leave hotels to find the bender,

my city's refineries in a city's blush
aslant. This rhino's not sullen, big,

pounding mystery or even diction
when the wanderer slips his plumb,

dumb luck some care. Bottoms up,
polished fast, then as the apparition

who dropped fully for dark streams
slurring. Backwards might I amuse

& tail between my legs, horn slung,
ballooned in diamond kiddie pools

please. Each city has its hero & I am
not him worried at the wide mouth

of bottles spinning, the juggled life
where an everyone edges erratically

for idioms bred into spring. Forever
& a day yielding its impulse, listing

dazed, I tramp this dandy imitation
to feed the dead ringer I've become.

Poem for James Shea

Nebraska keeps many lakes & I am
the face inside the rain, other rain

passing despite its lingering smell,
labor of cloud, infective sidewalk

where the city's steeples disappear.
Even so, someone smears the lens

for atmosphere & I'm pronouncing
yesterday confused, how it remits

shade & its sirens, secludes gravity
in the ladder that strands the roof.

Playing, yes, shy of a net, crossing
perilous streets when not marked

crossing. I'm implying if Nebraska
tapers murky, downshifts in ways

point A to B to Z, then burdened
through an image blurred so much

even sand adheres in water falling,
steady as the rocks I throw for you.

Anecdote of the Douglas Fir

What the girl he dreams from high school
said, having slept over though she hardly

ever spoke, never in fact went on a date,
he has no idea. O that hair, Sweetheart

bony-armed & beautiful, leaving campus
at lunch where she'll commit whatever

but volleyball. She is a mod bird, genius
who can't pull chatter together with glue.

Because he won't, how he nearly lifts her
like a fawn instead of dreaming that boy

who managed nearly not to hurt anyone.
At night in the lawn her best friend wept.

Requiem as Seen from Infinite Space

Isn't living plain enough, hankering
unavoidable, stealing with it a yard

& the spitting carbon of everywhere
you need to be today. Happier thrum,

twining until we batten the soft top
& miss the nice church luring old age

graciously, convincingly, reasonably
as a cornfield on a hot summer day.

You swerve the car often, see dodos
dragging twice their size. Breaking

for these abodes are the blue pools,
pairs of the clean wing & its horizon.

Let us weigh what dazzle we know
where our people reassemble & rise.

Upon the Patrons of the Game

We glove snow in our seats, confines
where men still usher spring, blossom

& brighten the sunlit weeks. Play ball,
threads held red by the imagined hands,

stitching & seams, the players younger
than most who stand inside the cheers

of popped fly balls, bullpens & mound.
To speak easily of pastime is our crime,

of sailboats, sliced apple pie, the trains
like foppery, no nonsense battle cries

interjected as the crowds shrill, gather
steam for peanut shells, candy & beer.

Autographs & souvenir, a healthy dose
of singing, we are the count on three.

It's April then July. We have no work,
no pledge in the morning. We implore

the win, we hope for flags blowing out,
days that flicker & shine, day that blinds.

Anecdote of the Western Hemlock

Neatly disappearing in a deep end
once, forgetting few & the flowers

I love. Names spilled from books
read in earnest until the afternoon

friends loaded cars in New Mexico
& Kalamazoo. Necessity dissolves,

mortality loiters cool, a hundred
percent sipping beer in the corner

over an empty dish. Wary friends
stayed honest in low paying jobs,

married sweeties & settled down.
I read the dispatch, leafed my own

on Sundays. Most of them letters
to the future tense, plans matched

& followed as if they added whole.
It was hard now & then to set aside

habit for ousting, wonted borough
in which I lived, maybe twice lived.

Once I nearly drowned & learned
to scrap thought for panic. Friends

built darkrooms in their basements,
friends whet appetites for cooking.

Travel was also being, & we loaded
cars for Seattle, Houston, Chicago.

Hurt & Hate Go Hand in Hand

Drove for a town of small reluctance,
another dance doubtingly. The folks

bid us forget their festivals nearing
& cheered, a happiest place to praise

ordinariness. Lethargic, you weren't
abnormal in the sinking hues. I was

ticketed, stubbed in some Naugahyde
asleep. Dreamt of a friend, laughter

rearranged like too much furniture
despite tea & its spoonful of gladness.

For you I'm able, explaining clumsily
rhythms & bone, nosebled histories

& last night was relative. It was tame
where you guessed fleece as a final act.

Given a chance, I'll tell you all about
my ugly & my ugliness. My uglinesses.

III

Like Fingernails Across the Moon

Careless clouds as opposed to science,
method in the ribcage & my breakfast

by the horn. A panic sung elsewhere
today, sequenced, inflected & mute.

I too can be the expert of horse flesh
when I wanna. Ahead lies the horizon

stamped as I choose to wed sensitivity,
mouth bon voyage for the very thing

I'd do for a hundred dollars. Intention
cores a thought, oh I forgot & abused

my haven, my passage, found myself
squared, honed inside a checkerboard.

The skylines flit in astraphobic pomp,
whimpering as I am that exaggerated

overcast, tripping glumly & catalogued
& thunderful. A window pushes open

to surely hear what's too dark to read.
Saying farewell is my least favorite part.

An Ounce of Prevention

The soldiers hurrying past you
stow a leather briefcase. There

rests a file thick, bearing names
where midnight scours a valley.

You swear for rabbits, rockets,
stretch the pedal floored. You

burrow books & comb feelings
inversely to the heart, pillbox

& flesh, pages buzzed into rage.
Likewise filed the full moon set,

men aged by their work & lean
for weather wends accordingly

to hear the bugle sound. You've
injured those dearest, your hair

again the odd wing descending.
In the end you'll be memorized.

Anecdote of the Royal Palm

As the plastic barrel chokes & pours,
better I welcome the cage, if I must

enticing that air I might like a whore.
Pulsating ribs, I hold my breath as if

straddling the well between blue sky
& bedrocks of orange petals strewn.

Debutante, mattress inside my shed,
they force me to the rodent's wheel.

My reds accrue in snare, hard chairs
pressing wrists over barb & beyond.

Grace in the blotting, glacial the nest
if the nude world ascends. My lungs

they fill, they take my beard instead,
lull me on the board, now & always

into hell. For this comfort I'm made.
If truth be told, I'll never be so alone.

By Any Other Name

Of what our motherhood warned
we forget, hedgerows & bramble

seeking or sought. Lost blunder,
bankruptcy when we chant songs

then tune each out with our ears,
chaperone of a barstool lending

relief. Or we faked a water wing,
showing & not telling our baskets

they're masquerade. Their stature
bears repeating for craftsmanship,

equal as the oats among our teeth
where we soon furbished lemons,

peddled them roadside by the cup
& if we'd only let the lining stray

beyond the cumulus, we'd deliver
bread. As such, we attract gazelles

grazing in concert, keeping mum.
Stripes in the mirror of their coats,

some are middle age, ornamental
& some favor crates. We vacillate.

We stumble far enough to tremor
& solicit hunger, the pride of lions.

Poem for Heroes & Bayonets

Dinner on the battlefield was worse
than our play. You were the eggshell

& I was the stone. You were buried
to the neck & the tide was inching in.

I signed the check, our waiter dashed.
It was no check but a contract, wires

coupled, strung to imminent crumbs
of the building swooned, the whoop

foretelling each pillar of arriving light.
Of our everyday life my least favorite

was the one in your head, brushwood
& edible, the hatchlings nestled there.

When men approached, your feathers
fell or flew. What was color if always

my zeroed knowns, those unknown,
& the voice releasing indelible things.

Anecdote of the Flowering Dogwood

Missouri runs late where language stands
beside the station at the end of a tunnel.

Missouri starves for a story. She's setting
out, suitcase on either side of the tracks

replete with fireflies for the tired cliché
blinks true. It bursts through darkness.

Language in that shine need not beguile,
transom opened by the rim of Missouri.

Animals take turns, boosted & gathering
about the brilliance of greenery spilled.

Language is useless as Missouri: she mates
sensibly, whispers the name of each city

& garlands, the sheer number of cardinals
breathless, naked atop the Missouri trees.

Most Likely to Secede

I am a room full of people. I am a room
facing people forward. What I've done

keeps me filled & I build myself taking
their heads. I wasn't hoping for a whorl,

rended for the era was one of undoing.
My people burned. My hospital burned

& burned. Birds went thump in the rays
like a stillborn crown, mainly baggage

where more burned inside the window.
Heat of so much clapping sang blisters

on my skin. I am a room full of people
who confess every millionth minor bird

& burn each one. Other, smaller birds
were birds left burning with their cribs.

Poem for Horses & Villains

We woke & named insects, thorn
& skulls. We incised time mowing

in a garden, tending tethered pets.
Their manners formed our voices.

Pedigree, fine huntsmen we were
not. Many trophied prey, in truth,

were our friends. By their example
we prayed each vision full, simply

our own wishbones doled & equal.
We kidded none & collected dust,

settled our dilemmas &, therefore,
were mutual loss. Our worst kind

grew brawn, so we forgave spring
or forgave fall. Along a stone fence

we waited days to swim. Otherwise
the cards were stacked in our favor.

We cracked among the yellow rose
& disaster. We were vespers for it.

We did not fool, not even in panic
or effect for our town was a stage,

our bridges like stations of a cross.
Our ghostly streets like presidents.

As the Light Enters & Registers

This poetry will not cap the well, this
but a test, figures & speech that loom

in streaks, the cadmium sea obsessed,
greased. Some clamor sickly, preening

wings & swallowing the trodden halo
of the reef. Wishing me less the image

pouring forth as the marshland frowns,
says goodbye & all this will be alright.

I am a lullaby convulsed much as I am
words changing color. A shoreline too

changing colors. This but my narrative
of the shoreline & word changing color.

Traveling in Pairs

Arm in arm in the advancing, striking
then struck into its science. Matches

bursting brightly & this match spent.
Every animal in the ark, a testimonial

to tango, what it takes to make a thing
go right. Blackened trees & lightning.

Heads or tails, good or evil just terrible
the age of two, lithium through neon.

Icons collapsing sisterly, Minneapolis-
St. Paul, sapphire tablets in either arm

stirring down a mountaintop. Trouble
doubling over, two & two put together.

Numeric standing in for doppelganger,
atom split, helium when our highway

delivers the northern tier. Superstition
akin to swagger. Awful, two-dollar bills.

The Tyranny of an Object

I shouldn't be so bared & lucky
was an excuse. Others included

my faith in institution, military
industrial thingy. Crashed a car,

staggered back upon the rubble
swept away. If there's revelry

I climbed a pole with abandon.
Married, but the ceiling leaked,

what was I thinking. I'd thought
how belief isn't the golden ring

you wear, but how you wear it.
I lacked the logic of flags flying

outside libraries, brimmed isms,
floor to ceiling stacks. I fancied

the knack in lose-lose situations
& then a horizon, & then the sun.

IV

Graced by a Certain Reluctance

I had numerous things growing up
& figured out. My left hand easily

chased perspective, multiplication
fed the number snug inside its box.

Mudflows bore cribs from houses
into bridges & I began to confound

such strange intuitions as audacity
with living. Scribbled in childhood

& sought praise, respect for letters
helped until the space shuttle blew

confetti everywhere. I was smarter
than a freeway south, mesmerized

under the billows of flattened cars
& temblors, then my constitution

took a liking to worry. I was ache,
reflexive, marooned the future life

to fathom how & when best friends
propelled their yards away for good.

Anecdote of the White Oak

Be beatific & stirring within ideas
where the blue waters diminish,

where feet & their transcriptions
emerge like secrets from a pond.

Or the white lily & resemblances
of a music piped to frenzy, rung

above the dead. Imminent speed,
lust & our loyalty on separate tabs,

lapping each other's faces & doing
so swiftly, intensely like Wagner

svelte, hubbub outside the fabric
of brown patience & photographs.

Pin morning to the ribbon boards,
distill the joy needled over weeks

& years, that wrist bone snapped
beneath my own arrested weight,

unforeseen. Cleanly, passing too
or the washrags tied into decency

sway goodbye aboard the seesaws
toward different seeing altogether.

Brief delight, a mallet lent to loss,
más o menos with pronunciation.

Like a flourish of branches backed
down a throat. Like a vast audition.

Debris of Caravans & Gold

Ardor, that newly picked flower,
nearly fits in our trousers. Opus

unfinished & this dialect we hope
eludes the stand of preciousness.

We censure every third machine
for the lonesome, slackened road

preceding us across the cemetery.
Grass, vanquish our jackets please,

fringe & warm the city. Blossoms
ease behind us, narrowed orama

until the prairie fits in our palms,
indifferent to the churn & crowds

plush with capital. A coyote lopes,
we hose our clothes late to school

except our calamities are plucked,
bobcats rummaging the dumpster

lean. We despise thrill & arcades,
ripple & glee on the pending shore.

Poem for James Shea

Nebraska has its panhandle & I am
sleeping politely. I am one of three

things lagging, a moustache drawn
fondly to brace the woman's nose.

I never cry pinched as the seconds
squander meaning. Words emerge

& rightly wither on a frozen hedge.
Sure I'll need to eat, spite landscape

in traffic & buildings. Between me
& me flows a skyway of vocabulary,

much as I am longing where armies
like Nebraska arrive & swell. I ply

laughter, act the whore I do believe
to be laughter. When April inhales,

I pinpoint my glass in that manner
cast over me, adored & betraying

particulars, many borrowed collars
beginning to curl, to smart, to singe.

Wooden Bridge & Wooded Waters

We had found our place in the sun
intending to saddle down. Took off

our jackets, our boots in the canyon
true west beneath the whirling falls.

Favor delivered dogs, whiskey sours,
the bride's brother & groom's sister

making out a little: her hiked skirts
of sorts, those steady mining efforts.

An hour is what was ours, the flood
& that explosion. We were the same

in our rare nakedness, tic-tac-toeing
necklines & breasts. There were no

better wishes for the coins we tossed.
Fig leaves were few in going around.

Anecdote of the American Elm

Near rivers & neighborly to a fault
as if he practiced smiling all his days,

waving the believable part, happier
than goddamn silliness. He forgave

himself of stubborn, longstanding
fluency. He matured, said buffoon

sweating spoons & rabbits hell-bent
past the funnel of his hat. He raised

certitude, stories of grinning valor
lest they disease, lest they diminish

evermore. Fences burst their beams,
rotted as rubble should, & so the he

he became rooted in common sense
& preceded the new common sense.

The Luxury of Sympathy

Knew a savior & with him my teen spirit
leaking gladness, juvenilia, what beauty

where I bend to magnify our brightest
star, harangue the worker ant & the hay

inside a kindled barn. Often in that track
I'm blind, owner & drone if what bows

doesn't break by the clamp & haul. Pails
bedded into recent America, lowering

rope & I floundered the well in falling,
exaggerate sickness, supposed torrents,

the five oceans hurled over the coastline
& into empty space. I was never prophet,

meant no phenomenal harm by my stare
deadpan, stumbled in books for a tense

deforested & gone trimming the green.
Today is cold, I'm not my thirties often

in the snow, in my wonder, once driven
high to spin in the mountain's darkness

toward the sun. Bewildered luminosity,
staggering likeness to the buzz trailing

my voice. I wished not to itch, vowed
to learn the biting comfort of my nails.

How to backpedal in light, its readiness
when this garden, minus love, succumbs.

Poem for Saplings & Semaphores

With the glassware, our silver flew
truthfully to the floor for somebody

must work around here. Their rage
set curfew to the early streetlights

near the trailer park. Dry lightning,
our fathers tended a field of tinder.

Waiting, we were scrum in that we
strayed, swore our lives rising too

beyond a flailing kite, out the door
from the poor defense of angry men.

We tied in time the pairing shrubs,
hammock & the yard far, far away

among the debris of distant moods,
milestones & mileposts for the night.

An Idea of Blossoms & Spring

Where crowds save face by removing
their faces. Save anesthesia & its letters

from a faraway nowhere. Where now
& its blankets drop, that It's-just-me

save the me I recollect restful & filled
with worthy old dreaming. My cannon

save fodder, confetti & homecomings,
pleasure ignited like a globe. Saving

sidewalks, save the white picket fence
& saintly pages thumbed, boys irking

rattlers in any case riled, noon amuck,
dillydallying. In my tree, pollenated

bees & force save firewood, rucksacks
ruined drunk by lions or shared. Like

apparitions bequeathed into a wallet.
The revolving cast. A surplus of seeing.

V

The Long Way Home

We ushered provisions. We bore
frontiers to ask what war was like.

By war vis-à-vis oil, & oil vis-à-vis
our asking how the aging wildlife

would survive. We were a secret
rallied by the halogen of the lamp.

Our handiness was well-renowned.
We roused time & wired our cots

for a raft. We advised immersion
& our mainsails were flimsy for it.

By immersion, vis-à-vis our souls
ordered change, floated up & wide.

We treated the month of Tuesdays
& forbid any other. We supposed,

in a serious way, we were godless.
Our symptoms were the following.

Poem for Saintliness & Marriage

Riffling great men who'd never
pick a fight, others who'd knock

to provoke the odds. Mirror me
for I've mourned a busted glass,

unearthed favors mute, patched,
packed in grass. Some hairlines

rapture & some nurturing spoils.
Some men are poor calculation,

shouldn't this suffice. Ordinarily
my drastic measure is the hunch

I'd give nearly nothing to abuse
some notable men, some dozing,

some dead. I fight to share a bed
dawning, curtained, nearly cured.

Anecdote of the Date Palm

As they shower me into blinding glare
or the load shatters my ribs, paralysis

like proof on that sun-splintered wall.
If I'd no slur in my tooth, this torment

would soothe inside my head the rabbit
wrung, dust stirring its wild frenzy up.

For every bulb hangs above like the day
in which teemed water, loosened first

the decoy inside my mouth. Semblance
of skin my words tore away, mistaken,

my memory graceless for these currents
wired to either finger, an anchor heavy

& cursing my ankle. Alphabet stricken
through the first ring of a newborn tree,

I expel this scenery to show my support
like a brick, the calf fattened with hatred.

State of the Union

Defeat doesn't dry because of deeds.
Because the cup of rain is bled, lays

abysmal at the curb, defeat is weedy
& leniency is for the weak. Because

distance softens blows, our tedium
dulled by the hour beneath the hose.

Because of brandish. Because of sham
& self-esteem, seeming & zero sums.

Because graveyards shift & mothers
know best. Weedy because of daring.

Because boys will be boys & bearing
carries us to the footholds. Because

ours is not anomaly, the roundness
of cloud & whimper facing its storm.

Because this callousness is supreme
given grouse get bored getting shot.

Because we grasp as much. Because
of curfew & streetlamps & the sound

doors sound when slammed. Because
we don't sanitize our very dilemma.

Because we greet ideas when defeat
rouses thirsty & tumbled & crowned.

Enough to Poison the Heart

Liken this compliment to the sway,
red rubber ball in the hold of a ship,

the captain drunk. You're innermost
before my articulation, transgressor

who steers this stern afoul & floods
the airway's flue. What ruins remain

per chance, what else closes for a fist.
I bereave lightning & so & so singing

in the vein. If you cannot sense land,
only sea, then leeward stars fly clean,

curious & arcane. I lessen & lessen
incessantly, bewildered under shapes.

That robin egg in the sky like a lung...
Come now, this world is mostly lung.

Feeding a Body to the Mountaintop

Animals resumed grazing, all engine
& aftermath. Or the cry of spouses

gagged, steeped, flung aside blindly
into the threshing core. Minds awry,

each trembles with muscle, arching
the other cheek or each oversleeps,

burdens collapsed. Infancy warrants
attention & stamina, moral authority

for those strings that tug are tugging
literally, memory reeled to the crater

of the molding fields. Sutures abide
if living can mother a failed coupling

no more at the gate of disparate shine.
None might expect a marriage twice,

half cell & half sheen by the remnant
of many leaving the loved one readily,

sad luggage, then bounded as though
through a thorn bush to retrieve a toy.

Anecdote of the Loblolly Pine

Twilight as in hushed, upstream
what began done rots the mud

hot & humid, the skeletal view
hollow in due course & mapped.

A field mouse in the night invites
permission, passage safe & straight

from swooping wings. Drought,
this old season's bed cracks paths

when cataracts flood, dizzy twigs
& blossom sprigs in the deluge.

It's heavily bankrupt news, deer
cornered, credence high-beamed,

carried south on turnpikes away,
downstream, tangled in the brush.

Poem for Pennants & Bunting

Empathy rose like a series of icebergs.
We were distracted. Linens needed

revisions, we realized a few desserts
would go uneaten, remain untouched.

When we parked the truck, the truck
got towed. This happens almost daily.

We walked the tracks circling town,
otherwise we might be screwed. We

brushed imperfect teeth: we squeezed
big tubes of paste into the little tubes.

We were the seven o'clock numbers
& we were making air. We stargazed

women coming & going in narratives
paired, walked in bars toward a joke.

Our friends had other, closer friends,
convictions, frost advisories in effect.

What we knew as cold, yellow tape
was a crime scene, the ex-boyfriends,

our bodies dragged on county roads.
We were figurines & were destroyed.

Lamplight & rotgut, our days passed
without thinking once about that war.

Every Thousand Years

Minutes whirl & wear me. I barely
write it down for the awkward lark

churrs lonely, accumulates a house
not under heaven. Purr or hummed

if you notice daffodils & helicopters
groan, fires blushing wrong hillsides

becomingly alive, beautiful in time.
Sprout & spray from the expired coil

enshrine this melted watch. Elation
upheld, even handsome in blooming

when multitudes celebrate & green
curls to renew our lives, lifting up

timber, blunting hatchets as if to say
I'll heed if for you & merely for love.

The Passionate Scarecrow

Cleaner than seeds that germinate
& split swagger by twos. Epochs

pass, these cherries persist to last
until plenitude yields but a stem.

Fathers & crimson sons dissuaded
of tenderness, of crying negligence

national & marital. Faces on coins
hardened, gemstones in the ring.

Fearless light, tired flies beyond
orchards, then the ghost crossing

the prairie home, wandering tall
as a fallen wood & lagging shadow.

Captions & corresponding mouths,
chucked with holes shot through.

A traveler's glove hung with bark.
Flags standing red on a county road.

Like So Many Mice in a Bucket

Wagons arrived uninvited, introduced
flora & fauna to spade & powder keg.

They mended fences & tested smoke
inside a cage. Praises as well cascaded,

set in postmodern patterns. My plans
held their ground with glue, balanced

& threaded & soon dropped in dimples
for middle age. I made like a blindfold

over the lip-synched history, led horses
to waterboards but couldn't make them

shrink. Not a secret plan, no thimbling
where the droplet vanished into grain.

The sky overhead was green, the land
blue, owls flew in storms approaching.

We eyed a haunted presence on behalf
of pining. My own heart lit & remained.

Winners of the Saturnalia Books Poetry Prize:

Neighbors by Jay Nebel

Thieves in the Afterlife by Kendra DeColo

Lullaby (with Exit Sign) by Hadara Bar-Nadav

My Scarlet Ways by Tanya Larkin

The Little Office of the Immaculate Conception by Martha Silano

Personification by Margaret Ronda

To the Bone by Sebastian Agudelo

Famous Last Words by Catherine Pierce

Dummy Fire by Sarah Vap

Correspondence by Kathleen Graber

The Babies by Sabrina Orah Mark

Also Available from saturnalia books:

Steal It Back by Sandra Simonds

Industry of Brief Distraction by Laurie Saurborn Young

That Our Eyes Be Rigged by Kristi Maxwell

Don't Go Back to Sleep by Timothy Liu

Reckless Lovely by Martha Silano

A spell of songs by Peter Jay Shippy

Each Chartered Street by Sebastian Agudelo

No Object by Natalie Shapero

Nowhere Fast by William Kulik

Arco Iris by Sarah Vap

The Girls of Peculiar by Catherine Pierce

Xing by Debora Kuan

Other Romes by Derek Mong

Faulkner's Rosary by Sarah Vap

Gurlesque: the new grrly, grotesque, burlesque poetics edited by Lara Glenum and Arielle Greenberg

Tsim Tsum by Sabrina Orah Mark

Hush Sessions by Kristi Maxwell

Days of Unwilling by Cal Bedient

Letters to Poets: Conversations about Poetics, Politics, and Community
edited by Jennifer Firestone and Dana Teen Lomax

Artist/Poet Collaboration Series:

Velleity's Shade by Star Black / Artwork by Bill Knott
Polytheogamy by Timothy Liu / Artwork by Greg Drasler
Midnights by Jane Miller / Artwork by Beverly Pepper
Stigmata Errata Etcetera by Bill Knott / Artwork by Star Black
Ing Grish by John Yau / Artwork by Thomas Nozkowski
Blackboards by Tomaz Salamun / Artwork by Metka Krasovec

In Memory of Brilliance & Value was printed using the font Perpetua.

www.saturnaliabooks.org